Meditation For Be

How to Meditate, Remove Negative Thinking, Stay Calm And Achieve Life-Long Peace

Theodore Maddox

Table of Contents

Introduction

Meditation has the capability and potential to completely alter your life, if done properly. This books purpose is twofold. It is designed to convince you that meditation is something that you should immediately implement into your life and to teach you the fundamentals of proper meditation techniques. As a long time psychiatrist, I can tell you with confidence that EVERYONE can benefit from daily meditation. People have a tendency to wind themselves up so tightly that they eventually 'snap.' Meditation allows you to slowly unwind yourself over time and to show you how to soothe your mind so that you never wind yourself up too tightly ever again.

This book has not been written with the intention to 'tell' you how you should be meditating, but rather to offer you helpful suggestions that you can either chose to implement, or not. The key to meditation is to keep in mind that it is an entirely personal experience. Nobody can tell you that you're meditating the wrong way. Everyone meditates differently and that is totally fine. Meditation merely serves as a means to an end; that end being a calmer demeanor, less overall stress and a more peaceful mind. It really doesn't matter how you get to that end, so long as you eventually get there. For some, achieving more peace in their life may only happen if they go skydiving once a month, giving them an adrenaline rush that calms them down overall. I know this sounds counterintuitive, but this is personally one of the things that I do to calm myself down. I find that after a major adrenaline rush everything else in life seems less important. Since you're reading this book though, I assume that your interest is not in skydiving, but in meditation. Along with skydiving once a month, I meditate twice a day, no matter what. My sessions last for about 15-20 minutes and they really make a difference in my life. I recommend meditation to all of my patients and many of them have seen great success with this practice.

I believe that the main reason that people don't see success with meditation is because they don't fully commit themselves to a strict meditation schedule, and when they do meditate they don't allow themselves to get lost in the experience. To have successful meditation experience we must shut off all distractions, including cell phones and computers! Meditation is an ancient practice and why do you think that it has endured for so long on this planet? Because it truly works wonders on mental and physical wellbeing. Meditation will make your life better if you do it all the time. In my opinion, the best part about meditation is that it's free and literally anyone can start doing it immediately. The human mind is a vastly powerful tool, it has the power to enhance us, or destroy us.

Mastering your mind is easier than you think if you're willing to put the time in. By meditating frequently you allow yourself to become more familiar with your mind. This may sound strange since you might think that you are already familiar with your mind, but think again. Modern life has become so non-stop and busy that most of us have no time to really relax. Most people's idea of relaxing involves watching television shows, listening to music and other similar activities. While these activities may be fun, they are not making you a more mindful person. For the majority of people, the only time they spend alone with their own thoughts is the few moments before they drift off to sleep. Have you ever woken up after a dream and felt like you were totally refreshed and that you had all the answers to the questions you had? That is what meditation can do for you everyday if you master the art. Allow me to take you through the fundamentals of the magical art of meditation. Your true peace and happiness is right around the corner!

Staying calm in stressful situations can be incredibly difficult. We are plagued with daily amounts of stress each and every day. Stress can have an impact on all aspects of our lives. Unfortunately, when we are faced with a great deal of stress, we usually do not know how to deal with these situations. Certain situations may occur within our lives that not only provide us with an immense amount of stress, but they can leave long lasting scars as well. While minor stress is normal, if you're facing large amount of stress that affects your daily life, you must find ways to reduce this stress. For some, the solution for dealing with stress may be different than others. Some individuals may choose to visit their local healthcare physician and request anti-anxiety and antidepressant medications. While these medications will numb you and not let you feel the same amount of stress that you may have been feeling before, you should not immediately turn to medication for relief. Luckily, there are other natural alternatives that can and should be used in place of harsh, chemical filled medications. You want to fix the problem at the source; you don't want to cover the problem up by numbing your feelings. Band-Aid solutions will only get you so far until the true problem rears its ugly head. Alternatives such as healthy vitamins, working out and meditation and other natural remedies are great solutions for stress, anxiety and depression. Mentally exercising your mind through meditation also helps decrease anxiety, stress and depression symptoms in a healthy and controlled manner.

There are basic fundamentals of meditating that must be followed. These fundamentals include but are not limited to; freeing your mind from thoughts and worries, sitting in a comfortable position, finding a quiet space, breathing deeply and focusing. Meditation is in fact a mental exercise that allows an individual to focus on one stimulus, whether that is a word, a place, an individual, a feeling or nothingness. A person must remain still during meditation and keep their mind focused on one thing. Part of the reason why meditation works so well with anxiety and depression is because it helps one gain control. When an individual is plagued with an anxiety disorder, they often do not feel that they are in control. These individuals do not feel that they are in control of their own feelings, actions, or the world around them. For example, a person with an anxiety disorder may be very afraid to fly but they choose to do so anyways. Once in the air, they may begin to have a panic attack.

During this panic attack there are a million thoughts that will be going through their head. One of these thoughts may be that they are not in control of the plane. What if they want to get off the plane? Well, they can't because the plane is in the air and the only way down is to land. What if they freak out and cause a scene with the other passengers and flight attendants because they are unable to control their own emotions? These are all thoughts that may go through an individual's mind who has an anxiety disorder. The lack of control is what really makes this into a very overwhelming disorder. When you're anxious, your heart rate often speeds up and your blood pressure rises as well. With meditation, in time, you will be able to teach yourself how to stay calm in all situations. Learning meditation techniques that can be used daily is incredibly helpful for those who suffer from anxiety as they start to feel more in control over situations when they are able to control what happens inside their bodies. Meditation not only benefits people with mental disorders but it can be an amazingly helpful addition to anybody's life!

When you panic, you lose control. You may start to hyperventilate, you may sweat, your heart rate will go up and you will not be able to think correctly. Meditating can actually teach you how to control your thoughts and your body perfectly. When you're taught new ways to control your emotions and automatic thoughts, you're less likely to have a panic attack. Panicking often leads to thoughts of death, dying and other thoughts that are abnormal and often, highly unlikely. Will this plane crash? Will I die of a heart attack today? What if I go blind when I'm driving home and I crash? These are all irrational but real thoughts that a person with anxiety may start to think about during a panic attack, or on a daily basis. Once you become aware of how to replace your negative thoughts full of worry and fear with positive thoughts, the amount of panic attacks and general stress that you have will go down significantly. Eliminate the unhealthy thoughts full of danger and fear with positive thoughts and actions through meditation tools. Meditating daily will help prevent panic attacks and will lower your daily stress levels as well.

We often become so overwhelmed with life that we forget to slow down. When we can't slow down, we take a pill for that. We take a pill in order to get a good night sleep but when we wake up and don't have any energy, we take a pill for that as well. Learning meditation techniques can eliminate unhealthy drugs from your life and encourage you to live a healthy lifestyle. Once you start meditating, you may then want to eat better and start exercising more as well. Personally I don't like doing a morning workout until I have done at least 10 minutes of meditation. Incorporating a healthy diet with meditation and a great workout routine is the best recipe for a healthy mind, a healthy body, and a healthy soul. Gain control of your life through meditation and eliminate negative thoughts and energy.

When you meditate, you can observe yourself. You can really think about yourself as a whole person. This type of introspective evaluation is incredibly important for personal and professional development. Whatever we want to accomplish or achieve can happen as long as we put our minds to it. Meditation encourages us to desensitize ourselves from any negative thoughts or restraints that we may have. Any fear, worry or concern can be eliminated from our lives through meditation. Instead of taking a trip to the doctor for a prescription, grab a mat, find a quiet place, focus, breathe and learn how to relax. You will be surprised at what can be accomplished when you simply put your mind to something and focus deeply without any outside distractions or unhealthy thoughts. Detach yourself from any negativity in your life and learn how to handle situations appropriately through self-evaluations and observations. When we understand what we're doing and why we're doing it, it becomes easier for us to eliminate these negative actions from our lives. Do not be consumed and overwhelmed by your problems. Understand them and eliminate them.

Focus! Focus! Focus! Even if it's on nothing. No matter how hard we try, sometimes it often becomes incredibly difficult for us to focus on what's in front of us. That being said, when we're trying to meditate, this problem can definitely put a damper on the process. The goal is to either free your mind from any and all thoughts, whether they be positive or negative, or to strictly focus on positive thoughts. When you're focused and calm your life will be enhanced, it's really that simple. Do not go through life constantly stressed out and under pressure when you don't have to. While you may feel overwhelmed at times, like there's no way out, luckily, there is.

There are a few fundamentals involved with the process of focus and meditation, the first thing you want to do is make sure you're getting a significant amount of sleep each night. Now, this is obviously easier said than done. We have children, we have to work late and sometimes we even have insomnia. Developing a better sleeping cycle will help you be a well-balanced individual overall. Some people survive off of coffee and energy pills to keep going and keep pushing through the day however these alternatives are not always the best or the healthiest solution out there. Meditation can not only teach you how to focus but it can also increase the amount of energy you have throughout the day.

When you start to meditate on a daily basis, it becomes more routine. It also becomes easier to meditate when you incorporate it into your daily schedule. The more you meditate, the more effective the process is. If you tried meditating once and it was difficult for you, that's ok. It takes time for us to acquire the necessary skills when trying to have a healthy meditation experience. In order to meditate effectively, there are a few steps that must be followed in order to achieve the full effect of meditation and the remarkable things that it can do for our mind our body and our soul.

Getting plenty of sleep, as discussed before may be difficult but it's definitely doable. Luckily, we're able to focus more with little sleep when we're younger. When we get older however, this often changes. Once we enter into adulthood, if we want to truly be productive in life we must focus on getting an adequate amount of sleep as many nights out of the week as possible. Getting between seven to eight hours of sleep at night is usually best. Keep in mind that you don't want to sleep less than seven-eight hours, or more than seven- eight hours because too much sleep can affect you in a negative way as well. It may be difficult for some of us to achieve this and sleep for this amount of time.

We have children, snoring partners, and other disturbances that we may be faced with at night. Ensuring that we receive an adequate amount of sleep each night is crucial for the meditation process. Finding time to sleep is difficult but you must either set yourself a bed time, or find time during the day to take naps when trying to make up for lost sleep hours at night. However you make up for it, make sure you're sleep patterns are in sync, consistent and effective.

Eliminating distractions is another important aspect of meditation. Meditation is all about relaxing. Meditation leads you to find peace within yourself and within your mind. If there are loud noises, loud conversations, or other things going on around you, it's going to be very hard to focus. While you're meditating try to stay in the zone. You have to lose track of what's around you. Turn your phone off and any TV's that may be around and just get lost in yourself.

When you are able to tune out the world, you will begin to truly understand yourself. Find your zone. Do not think about time, space, what's for dinner or cleaning the house, get lost in the moment of meditation. We often become so busy with our normal lives and routine that clearing our minds is incredibly difficult. When we focus on life, school, our children, work and other things that take up our time and energy, it's hard to let these thoughts go, even if it's only for a short amount of time.

One way to encourage meditation is to perform the activity a few times per day. Now, I know this may seem extreme, but it's not. Meditation usually requires a significant amount of time, say 10-20 minutes or so, that being said, it doesn't have to. When we transfer ourselves from one area of our lives to another, it becomes difficult for us to process this. For example, when we leave work and go straight into mommy/daddy or wife/husband mode at home, we may feel overwhelmed, like the work just never stops. Try taking a few minutes after each daily transitional phase to meditate. Short amounts of meditation can be done during this time. Take a few minutes and leave the work persona behind, gather your thoughts and let that part of your day go completely before you enter into your next transitional phase.

Work alone can be incredibly overwhelming. We must find time in our day to look over our work day and then look forward to what's in store for us at home. That being said, you must give yourself that time in between the transitional phase to gather your thoughts and process your next steps. When an environment changes, so do our thoughts, feelings and actions. This time can be used to leave behind any negative energy that may have been developed at work, and start fresh with the new transition. Try taking the time while you're commuting to and from work to let go of any negative energy. If you're on your way to work, try not to think about the argument you just had with your significant other that morning or what you need to do once you get home. Free your mind of any thoughts, that way you are able to start your workday with a clean slate.

Try thinking about positive and healthy places while you're driving. This is your zone. Your zone can be anything from a deserted island to a quiet cabin in the mountains. This action is referred to as visual meditation. When we are able to visualize an idea or place and focus solely on that place, this is considered visual meditation.

This type of meditation is effective as it allows us to picture and visualize in our minds what we want. We can either visualize a place where we want to be in life or maybe on vacation. Whatever and wherever this place may be, make sure it's a safe and healthy place full of peace and serenity. Whatever your zone may be, make sure you're able to free your mind when you're thinking about this beautiful place.

Quite honestly, you will have an incredibly difficult time meditating if you're unable to free your mind of daily thoughts. This is something that you must practice and it will take time. Be patient, in time you will train your mind to clear when the time is right.

Chapter 3: Environment is Everything

There are many factors that make meditating effective. One factor is the environment in which the meditation is occurring. It's important to remember that the meditation environment may be different for everyone. For example, some individuals may choose to meditate outside, some individuals will want to meditate while doing yoga in a yoga class and others may be able to simply plop down in their living room, turn the TV off and meditate. The entire process of mediation, while it involves many different factors, ultimately relies on the environment where the meditation is taking place. You most likely will not see an individual in the middle of Disneyland meditating. You might, but the likelihood of this happening is very low. The first thing you need while meditating is a quiet place. This quiet place can be anywhere you feel comfortable. Do not let distractions get in the way of your meditation process. Most individuals need a quiet area free of other distractions and individuals in order to really get into the meditation process. Whether it's your family or friends, dog or cat, distractions can and most likely will, get in the way of your stress free meditation session.

If you really want to encourage the distraction free meditation environment, discuss this with your family, friends, roommates, or whoever else may disrupt the process. Setting a certain time out of the day to meditate is a great start to this. If you have a roommate for example, let her/him know that every night at 8:00PM you'll be meditating. If needed, place a do not disturb sign on the door if you feel they might forget. When you set expectations and you're proactive when setting the stage for your meditation techniques, you are more likely to reach your goal. Now, that being said, keep in mind that you can make all the arrangements in the world and still not be able to control everything that happens. You may be on a great meditation cycle when your neighbor decides to throw a party at 8:00PM with incredibly loud music and a lot of people. Now, if that happens, it's ok, you may not be able to get through a full meditation session that night, so just make sure you squeeze some time for meditation into your morning the next day to make up for it and unwind.

Another approach to something like this happening is to try and tune out the outside noises. This is a true test of how well you're able to meditate and shut out the rest of the world. It may not be possible for everyone to do this, no matter how long you've been meditating but it's worth a try. Try focusing on your breathing and your inner thoughts and tune out the outside noise. You may find that you are able to meditate through all the noise and crazy partying going on next door! Keep in mind that this will take a great deal of focus and concentration and you may not be at this level yet. If you're not at this level, that's ok, at least you tried! In time, you will be. If you want to you could even seek out a noisy environment on purpose to truly test you meditation skills.

Once you are able to eliminate the majority of noise and disturbances around you, the next thing you want to do is identify a specific meditation area where the meditation will be taking place. Now, this ideal place will be different for all individuals, but there are some common guidelines that you may follow. For example, having a clean area where you meditate. It's important to remember that meditation involves freeing your mind and body from anything that may be preventing movement or blocking you from other things. If the space that you're in is dirty and cluttered it will be hard to unclutter your mind if what you're looking at is full of clutter as well. That being said, you don't need to scrub the area on your hands and knees every day, however, it's important to keep the area clean and tidy.

Keeping your place clean and organized helps keep your mind organized and clear as well. While you may not be able to control your living situation, you can however clean up after yourself and others to ensure that you're living in a reasonably clean area. The goal of mediation is to clear negative ideas and energy out while balancing your mind, body and soul. That being said, decluttering your mind also involves decluttering your house or living space as well. If you're trying to look for a spot to sit on the ground and meditate and you can't because of the overwhelming amount of dirt and trash on the floor, well, this is definitely a problem. That being said, while most individuals will sit on the floor to meditate, you can actually sit anywhere as long as you're comfortable, because comfort is key! If you're not comfortable, you will not be able to focus and really search within yourself. If you're uncomfortable physically, you won't be able to be comfortable within either. I personally have a small cabin down by the water and I have dedicated this place to being my meditation zone. Try to be consistent with your meditation zone, as this will enable you to relax as soon as you get yourself into your chosen environment.

While meditating, some people may choose to sit with their legs crossed, otherwise known as the lotus pose, or you can simply sit on a sofa, bed or chair. Wherever you sit, you must be comfortable enough to stay in that position and keep your mind in that position as well. If you're comfortable you'll be able to focus on what you're feeling within, you won't be focused on what you're feeling on the outside. It's very important that you choose comfort over trying to do what everyone else does. If you're comfortable on the couch and not on the floor, but you've seen most other individuals meditating on the floor, it doesn't matter! Do what's best for you. As long as your body is comfortable, you can meditate anywhere. Seeking to eliminate as much external stimuli as possible is a vital part of meditation.

If you are lucky enough to have an extra room, try turning it into your own meditation room. Make this space your worry and stress free zone. Whatever negative thoughts or feelings you have, leave them at the door and do not let them enter into this room. Adding candles, aroma therapy and soft scents such as lavender and sage will bring peace and a sense of calmness to the room. While this may not be possible for all of us, if you are able to have a meditation room the first thing you want to do is make sure it's the cleanest room in your house. If you are fortunate enough to have an extra room, do not start using this room as a storage area for your junk, this must be a junk free room. It must be an open space where you can enter into a state of concentration so deep that nothing else will matter.

Keep in mind that while yes, you want the space to be clean, you also want to make sure that you have all the necessary meditation items in the room as well. The first thing you'll need (if it's comfortable for you) is a yoga mat. You can buy a yoga mat just about anywhere nowadays and they aren't too expensive. Yoga mats come in all different colors and textures so find one that's suitable for you. Before you buy the mat, try sitting on it to ensure that it is comfortable. If you like, and you can afford it, buy a few yoga mats so that you can alternate and find which one will work best for you. The type of yoga mat that you'll buy will ultimately depend on the type of meditation that you're doing. For example, if your specific form of meditation involves a specific type of yoga such as Bikram Yoga, make sure the mat you purchase is for Bikram Yoga. You don't want to try and do Bikram Yoga on a regular exercise mat. While it's possible, it isn't going to make the experience very positive. When it comes to meditating, you want to make sure you're following all the right steps. Check out any sports store or look online to compare prices and find the best mat for you! But as stated before, you don't need a mat if you choose to meditate on a couch or bed, etc.

Now, let's look at the temperature of your room. The first thing you want to do is make sure your temperature is somewhere around 70 degrees. The goal here is to make sure that the temperature isn't too hot or too cold as this can be distracting. If you're trying to meditate and you're freezing in the room, you won't be able to concentrate, you'll only be able to think about grabbing a sweater and bundling up. If the room is too hot, this will be a frustrating distraction as well.

Set the thermostat at a comfortable temperature and make sure that it remains there. Along with temperature, check the lighting in the room as well. Try leaving the room with natural lighting, as a major part of meditating is feeling as though you're one with nature. Natural light should be more than enough light to meditate with. If you're meditating at night, make sure that you have a small amount of lighting in the room. You don't want to have the room so dark that you fall asleep and you don't want the room to be so bright that you feel as though you're under investigation. Keep the lighting like the temperature, somewhere in the middle and you'll be just fine. Just keep the word "calm" in mind and let that guide you when preparing your room.

Remember, with a sense of calmness comes clear and pure areas, free of décor and clutter. Meditation rooms do not need to be decorated. In order to create a more natural environment, try adding a speaker system into the room. Find a relaxing station with nature sounds and press play. Maybe you're listening to the waves at the beach or a stream running down the mountain, whatever it is, make sure it's calm and by that I mean, you don't want to try meditating to Jay-Z or Kanye's hit songs. Make sure the music is natural and peaceful and full of nature.

Focus on the clean, open space, perfect temperature and nature sounds and you'll be ready to meditate and find your inner self! Better yet, try meditating outside in nature. Outdoor meditation is a favorite among many people and I strongly advise you to try it. I find meditating by a river or the ocean to be the best place to go. The sound of the water moving becomes very soothing and it tends to block out any other potentially distracting noises in the area.

During meditation practices, breathing is everything. Learning how to properly control your breathing during meditation is crucial for successful meditation moments. Mediation is not simply sitting down and humming with your legs crossed. There is so much more to mediation that is required to really be able to receive the full effect of the technique. Breathing techniques are used to calm your entire body. Breathing meditation is used to find inner serenity and peace within your mind and soul.

The only way that meditation will actually work is to free your mind of distractions, focus and breathe. When our minds our free, we are able to breathe deeply. For example, when we are stressed out and under pressure, we tense up. When we're feeling tense, we are not able to breathe at a deep level. You first want to make sure that your posture is correct. If you're sitting down and slouching, you're not going to be able to inhale deeply. Find a comfortable position to sit in, sit up straight and start practicing your breathing technique.

The first thing you must do is turn your attention to how you're breathing. When you begin meditating, your focus is on your breathing. Deep belly breathing is important as it helps relax your body. Keep in mind that it's not going to be easy at first. You'll have to tune everything out in your environment, you'll have to free and clear your mind and only think and focus on your breathing. Focusing on our breathing is much easier said than done, especially for someone who is constantly busy and full of energy.

Meditating takes time and practice, specifically, learning how to breathe effectively takes time and it takes a great deal of practice. When you begin to focus on your breathing, you will start to become aware of just how many different thoughts run through your mind each and every day and every moment. We don't realize how many thoughts are in our minds until we try and tune them out. It will be difficult at first to not give into these other thoughts, in fact, it's very hard at first to not let your mind wander over to these thoughts, but in time you will be able to do this with little effort.

This is where a great deal of discipline comes into play. You must discipline yourself and your mind and remember that you're only focus at this time is the way you're breathing. If you find that your mind continues to wander off, start again. Start again as many times as you need until you are able to only focus on how you're breathing. Over time, this breathing practice will allow your distracting thoughts to subside.

You will not master your breathing techniques overnight. Breathing meditation is one of the first stages of deep meditation but it can be incredibly powerful. Immediately, once we are able to only focus on our breathing and we can eliminate all other thoughts from our minds, we will start to find inner peace. A great deal of our stress is created through our thoughts and fears. When we find ourselves focused on these thoughts and we meditate, focusing on our breathing and letting go of these fears becomes simple and we begin to gain more control over what comes and goes through our minds.

Finding a significant amount of deep contentment and happiness can be achieved just by doing ten minutes of deep breathing meditation each day. When we meditate and focus on our breathing we tend to feel more calm and relaxed. Letting go of unnecessary stressors through breathing meditation encourages a free and open mind that is not willing to allow negativity in. Health issues are often caused and or triggered by stress. Knowing that these issues can be avoided or eliminated through meditation should be a great incentive for people to focus on their meditation skills.

While you are practicing deep belly breathing the proper technique to use is, in through your nose (belly expands as you fill it with air), out through your mouth (belly deflates as you let all of the air out). Try breathing in for five seconds and out for five seconds. Do this for an entire minute and then do it again, this time breathing in for ten seconds and out for ten seconds. See how long you can breathe in and out for without panicking and losing your breathing pattern.

The key is to remain calm and ensure maximum air intake on the inhale so that you have a lot of air to expel once you exhale.

Once you get up to breathing in for thirty seconds and out for thirty seconds, you will likely find that it's becoming very difficult. Focus on staying calm and breathing in the most efficient way possible and with practice you'll soon be breathing in for one minute and out for one minute, or maybe even longer!

Transcendental meditation is common form of meditation that can be used to treat many different ailments. This type of meditation focuses on avoiding negative or distracting thoughts. You should ease your mind just by knowing that there are things that can be done in order to eliminate and reduce the symptoms associated with menopause. One way that menopause can be dealt with is through meditation.

Any and all individuals can use this type of meditation. It has had an immense amount of success in all areas and is also the most widely researched form of meditation today. A well-trained instructor usually teaches this type of meditation. In order to be a meditation instructor, you must simply love your craft and literally practice what you preach. Practice is key for this and any other type of meditation. Without practice, you will not be successful. One of the differences between this type of meditation is the fact that this type of meditation focuses on chanting rather than just visuals.

A mantra or visual is focused on in order to decrease stress, eliminate anxiety and work on self-development. There's a specific technique involved with transcendental meditation. The first thing you must do is sit with your eyes closed. Next, a mantra will occur for 15-20 minutes. This type of meditation has been viewed as both religious and nonreligious but continues to be practiced around the world. Learning how to complete this type of medication takes proper instruction. Choosing a mantra is a totally personal choice. There are many ancient mantras that you can choose from, here is a list:

http://mindbluff.com/mantra.htm

If those do not suit your fancy, fear not because you can create your own mantra. Maybe you have a favorite word or phrase that evokes peace and calmness in your mind. Experiment with different mantras, choose the one that works for you and repeat it constantly as you practice transcendental meditation.

An instructor of transcendental meditation must be a master in order to teach the practice effectively. This instructor's fees may vary based on the country where the process is being taught. For many, they are willing to pay whatever it takes in order to learn the tools of this type of meditation due to its overwhelming success. Individuals have been very successful with eliminating and decreasing their symptoms of stress and anxiety just by practicing this type of meditation. When we are overwhelmed with stress and anxiety, it can often take over our entire life to learn to cope with it, or perhaps never learn to cope. Specifically, if someone is facing a traumatic time in their life such as menopause, post-traumatic stress disorder, or anxiety, they are often in search of a way out. Individuals begin to search for a solution. Some women find themselves completely overwhelmed when they begin facing symptoms of menopause but meditating is a great solution for these symptoms! More specifically, transcendental meditation is an incredibly popular form of meditation that has been known for relieving menopause symptoms from women.

Practicing this specific form of meditation can eliminate fatigue and eliminate or reduce mood swings that are often associated with menopause. This form or meditation is also great because not only does it eliminate the initial symptoms that a woman may be facing but it also provides for a more enriching life full of an immense amount of content, clarity and energy. When we feel better about ourselves on the inside, it ultimately helps with our symptoms that we may feel on the outside as well. Transcendental meditation helps will all aspects associated with menopause. There are many other areas and ailments that be treated with this specific type of meditation. Specifically is the psychological aspect of menopause and other ailments such as anxiety, post-traumatic stress disorder, and ADHD just to name a few.

When someone is plagued with the pain and stress of post-traumatic stress disorder, this is often an incredibly difficult time in their life. Focusing on what's inside is the most important aspect of this type of meditation. Training your way of thinking is a huge focus as well. Specifically, children suffering from ADHD have a difficult time focusing. Children and adults are often embarrassed by their inability to focus on a topic or subject. Overtime, with transcendental meditation, this can be eliminated. When you practice on your focus, it will increase. Meditation practices like this help train your mind to only focus on what's in front of you. When we are busy, things often distract us very easily, for a person who suffers from ADHD, they are often consumed by daily distractions that are out of the norm. These distractions can cause a great deal of stress and other negative emotions. With meditation, you are able to teach yourself how to focus and become more aligned with your thoughts and what's inside.

When this point is reached, women begin looking in different areas for a new meaning in life. One way that this can be discovered is through meditation. Meditation forces an individual to look deep within and find their happiness. That being said, meditating takes you on a journey through your soul. When you look within, you discover parts of yourself that may not have been visible before. When meditation is done correctly and twice a day as recommended by most spiritual guides, you will find self-sufficiency, you will find a new self that is different than what you were before. When you know who you truly are as an individual, you are then able to develop more in-depth relationships with others. When we're younger, we are often so incredibly busy with lives, our children, developing our careers and taking care of our families that we lose our own identity. This identity often becomes lost because of our busy schedules and the overwhelming need to take care of others over taking care of ourselves. The only way to truly find ourselves is to look within and find our soul.

Transcendental mediation works by reducing anxiety levels and lowering stress. When the body learns how to let go of stress, instead of holding onto it, the other symptoms involved with menopause will ultimately start to decrease. Practicing this form of mediation for 20 minutes twice a day helps lower the stress hormone cortisol. When you're meditating, you're in a completely relaxed state, your body, mind and soul are all completely relaxed and your body then becomes familiar with this. When you are able to decrease the overall amount of stress that you have, your mood will be lifted and you will then be able to sleep better as well. As far as hot flashes, those occur when our body reaches a state of overheating, these hot flashes can increase sweating, your skin may be flushed and you will be incredibly hot. While the exact cause of a hot flash is unknown, what we do know is that learning how to keep circulation and the stress hormone cortisol at a low level, this will lower the chance of having a hot flash. Menopause can be a challenging time for many women. Menopause is a time of change, but that change can also create new opportunities and a new view and perspective on life. With transcendental meditation, you will learn how to cope with the stress and symptoms associated with menopause in a healthy way that will give you the tools to eliminate overall daily stress as well.

Transcendental meditation is good for all different types of ailments and issues. This meditation is incredibly successful and with the right amount of time and patience, you will certainly find success with this. Taking the time to practice this daily can make you a more successful person. You will not only be able to focus, but you will have less overall stress as well. Once you start practicing transcendental meditation, you will not want to live a life without it.

While it may seem as though there's only one type or form of meditation, this is simply not the case. For example, one form of meditation focuses specifically on increasing concentration skills. Concentrating is often easier said than done. It's hard for children and adults to focus at times. We often become distracted by other problems and issues and have trouble focusing on important issues. Keep in mind that during this form of meditation, you must train your mind.

The mind must be trained to either focus on nothing at all, or a specific object. The next type of meditation is reflective meditation. This specific form of meditation focuses on disciplined focus and thinking skills. The first step with this type of meditation is taking one topic, idea or question and fully analyzing this. The more you practice reflective meditation, less likely it will be that your mind will wander off and you will feel more in control. Reflecting on anything in life is important. When you are able to look back on your actions, choices and decisions, you can reflect on what you feel you did right and what you may have wanted to work on. Reflections, whether they be personal or professional reflections, are incredibly important for success.

Self-reflecting helps you improve overall. When you reflect on life, your meditation skills, or anything else, you are able to fix areas that need to be fixed and praise yourself appropriately as well. When you're meditating and using reflective meditation skills you can think about things such as identifying what your true purpose is in life, you can think about who you are as an individual and in different areas of your life. Maybe you're reflecting on your job title or thinking about how you can help others. Whatever it is you're reflecting on and thinking about, make sure you are not overwhelmed with your thoughts. Find one question to focus on during each session. If you focus on too many questions, you will not be able to come up with solutions to problems or questions that you have.

Heart-centered or chakra meditation is another popular form of meditation. When you have an overwhelming amount of fears or sadness, meditation that is focused on your heart can be incredibly powerful and helpful when trying to overcome these issues. This type of meditation helps you let go of your sadness and fears and welcome in nothing but love, peace and kindness. The heart chakra meditation will help you heal and protect your heart over time. The heart chakra is incredibly important in the world of meditation as it often holds on to negative energy. This negative energy is often filled with sadness and pain. When you meditate it helps open the heart chakra and then allows for energy that is negative to be released and it allows you to let go of these harmful and hurtful feelings. During this type of meditation, it is known to be most effective when you think about someone you feel strongly about while you meditate. Make sure whoever you think about is not causing you pain. You want to focus on someone positive in your life that you love and care about. Connecting your heart to this person mentally and emotionally will help free your heart of negative energy involving others.

Conclusion

Do not waste another moment of your time living a life that is without meditation. I challenge you to create a meditation schedule, stick to it and not feel like a completely rejuvenated person after only a few days. Not utilizing the art of meditation is a total waste of potential in my opinion. The mind is a powerful tool, but we need to stimulate it regularly if we want it to function in an optimal way. It is my sincere hope that you will begin to reap the benefits of daily meditation. I hope you enjoyed this book and I wish you all the best in your quest to a more peaceful, calm and fulfilling life that is filled with fantastic moments of deep meditation.

I honestly hope that you will apply what you've learned from this book to your daily life. It is one thing to read about a more enlightened life, but it's a different ball game when you start taking the necessary steps to enhance your existence. Be calm and prosper, for a stressed person is seldom a happy one.

CHECK OUT A PREVIEW FOR ANOTHER ONE OF MY BOOK TITLES ON THE FOLLOWING PAGE:

"ZEN PARENTS"

Introduction

Parenting, by far is the hardest job anyone can have. You can spend years parenting your children but it's often difficult to find the best parenting style for you and your children. Luckily, there are an immense amount of parenting skills than can be acquired over time. Learning how to be the best parent possible is incredibly important. It's important to remember that no matter what type of parenting situation you're in, you will find yourself being tested over time. The goal when you're being tested, is to handle situations in an effective manner in order to teach your children how to problem solve effectively. Be a role model for your children. Understand that children, although they are young can understand and feel everything around them. Show your children that it's ok to make mistakes, as long as you learn from them. Show them that the world is a beautiful place full of options and opportunities. Teach your children how to explore the world and not be afraid of it. Below you will find a few tips and tools that will help you during your parenting years. With the right tools, and the right attitude, you will be able to guide your child in the right direction, teach them right from wrong and encourage them to have empathy for others.

Parenting doesn't stop at the age of 18. It continues on for a lifetime. Keep in mind that while some tools may work at one stage of your child's life, you may not work later on. Learn from your parenting mistakes and keep growing and learning about yourself and your child. Most importantly, remember that no one is a perfect parent. No matter how hard you try, you will struggle at times with parenting. As long as you know that you're doing your best, and you're doing everything in your power to raise a healthy, happy, and well-mannered child, them that's all that matters. Learning how to listen, co-parent, deal with different behaviors and accept the fact that at some point you have to let your child go live his/her own life are all very important aspects of parenting. While these aren't easy tasks by any means, they are very important for effective parenting to take place.

Printed in Great Britain
by Amazon

37427986R00020